MW00909202

RONALD
REAGAN

40th US President

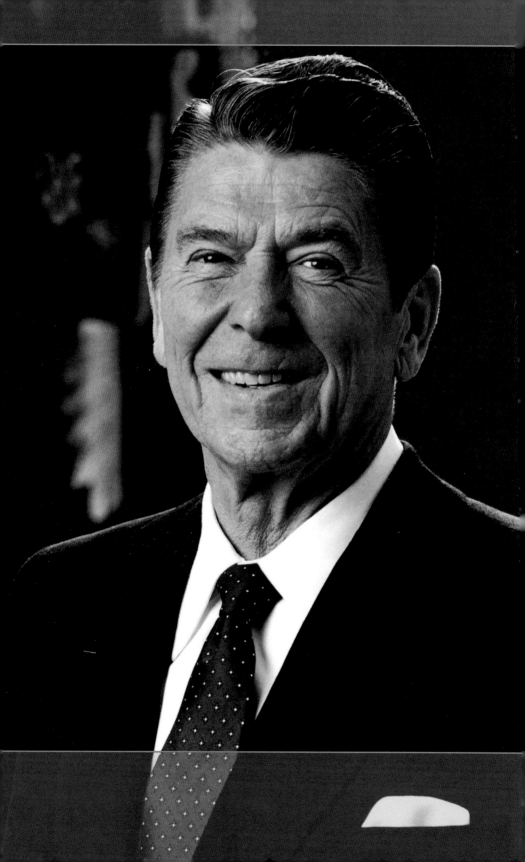

RONALD
REAGAN

40th US President

BY ROSA BOSHIER

CONTENT CONSULTANT
DIANE J. HEITH
ASSOCIATE PROFESSOR AND CHAIR,
DEPARTMENT OF GOVERNMENT AND POLITICS
ST. JOHNS UNIVERSITY

ABDO
Publishing Company

CREDITS

Published by ABDO Publishing Company, PO Box 398166, Minneapolis, MN 55439.
Copyright © 2014 by Abdo Consulting Group, Inc. International copyrights reserved
in all countries. No part of this book may be reproduced in any form without written
permission from the publisher. The Essential Library™ is a trademark and logo of ABDO
Publishing Company.

Printed in the United States of America,
North Mankato, Minnesota
052013
092013

Editor: Arnold Ringstad
Series Designer: Becky Daum

Photo credits: US Government, cover, 2; Bettmann/Corbis/AP Images, 6, 42, 49, 66,
68, 75; Bob Daugherty/AP Images, 11; Ira Schwarz/AP Images, 12; Bob Springer/
AP Images, 14; Reagan Library Archives, 17; AP Images, 21, 22, 29, 32, 37, 39, 45, 50,
58, 60, 64, 77; Eureka College Yearbook/AP Images, 25; CBS/Hulton Archive/Getty
Images, 53; White House, Michael Evans/AP Images, 72; Pete Souza/White House/
AP Images, 78; Mittelstaedt/AP Images, 80; David Hume Kennerly/Getty Images, 83;
Dennis Cook/AP Images, 85, 88; Mike Sargent/AFP/Getty Images, 87; J. Terrill/AP
Images, 91; Elise Amendola/AP Images, 93

Library of Congress Control Number: 2013932925

Cataloging-in-Publication Data

Boshier, Rosa.
 Ronald Reagan : 40th US President / Rosa Boshier.
  p. cm. -- (Essential lives)
ISBN 978-1-61783-895-8
Includes bibliographical references and index.
1. Reagan, Ronald, 1911-2004--Juvenile literature. 2. Presidents--United States--
Biography--Juvenile literature. 3. United States--Politics and government--1981-1989-
-Juvenile literature. 4. Motion picture actors and actresses--United States--Biography-
-Juvenile literature. 5. Actors and actresses--United States--Biography--Juvenile
literature. I. Title.
973.927/092--dc23
[B]   2013932925

CONTENTS

CHAPTER
ONE

THE SECOND INAUGURAL

It was January 21, 1985. On the day of President Ronald Reagan's second inaugural address, he stood in the Capitol Rotunda and looked out at a crowd of hopeful faces. They looked forward to a bright future under Reagan's continued leadership. Reagan's first term had its fair share of difficulties and challenges, but Americans had demonstrated they were still willing to stand by him for another four years. American voters connected with the president's promises of change, safety, and freedom, as well as his pledge to foster a new American self-confidence.

The cold winter weather had forced the inauguration ceremony indoors. For the first time, a president would take the public oath in the Capitol Rotunda. Overhead lights shone warmly on Reagan and his wife Nancy as they walked toward the podium. Chief Justice Warren E. Burger administered the oath of office to President

Like most presidents, Reagan placed a hand on a Bible during his swearing in.

Reagan amid the flash of cameras. After Reagan uttered, "So help me God" at the oath's conclusion, an artillery salute was fired off outdoors, the band began playing "Hail to the Chief," and the crowd erupted in applause. When the applause finally began to die down, the President approached the microphone.

After thanking the assembled officials, he reminded listeners of the nation's historic progress:

> When the first President, George Washington, placed his hand upon the Bible, he stood less than a single day's journey by horseback from raw, untamed wilderness.

WARREN E. BURGER

Warren E. Burger was born in Saint Paul, Minnesota, on September 17, 1907. After graduating from law school, he became a politically active lawyer in Minnesota. In 1955, President Dwight D. Eisenhower nominated him to be a federal court judge. When US Supreme Court Chief Justice Earl Warren retired in 1969, President Richard Nixon nominated Burger to his position.

Burger was involved in many important decisions during his time on the Supreme Court. These included the *Miranda* decision, which forced police to inform suspects of their rights upon arresting them, and the *Roe v. Wade* decision, which established women's rights to have abortions. Burger also presided over four presidential inaugurations, including both of Reagan's.

Burger retired from the Supreme Court in 1986, halfway through Reagan's second term. Upon his retirement, Reagan elevated Associate Justice William Rehnquist to the position of chief justice and nominated Antonin Scalia to take Rehnquist's place. Burger died in 1995 at the age of 87.

There were 4 million Americans in a union of 13 States. Today, we are 60 times as many in a union of 50 States. We've lighted the world with our inventions, gone to the aid of mankind wherever in the world there was a cry for help, journeyed to the Moon and safely returned. So much has changed, and yet we stand together as we did two centuries ago.[1]

A New American Hope

Reagan's words rang through the Capitol Rotunda as he spoke of uniting America and looking forward to creating a new beginning for the American people. He talked about government deregulation in the name of economic freedom. He championed the values of faith, courage, and love. He advocated the creation of a missile defense system that would make nuclear weapons obsolete. He spoke of ending unemployment, increasing equal rights, and protecting liberty. He tried to instill in his supporters the hope for a new American Revolution, a new birth of freedom future generations would see as a turning point in the history of the United States.

After Reagan spoke, the crowd again broke into applause. Following periods of political scandal and a difficult economy, many Americans finally felt the nation was moving forward. However, Reagan had a great deal of work ahead of him. He would face a balancing act between his personal values and the compromises needed to make progress. Yet after four years of presidential experience, Reagan entered his second term with confidence.

Public Opinion

In his second inaugural speech, Reagan painted a picture of a United States that was still strong and still growing. However, he also acknowledged the country had experienced a time of economic stress. Reagan's optimism during hard times helped him win votes. "We, the present-day Americans," he said, "are not given to looking backward. In this blessed land, there is always a better tomorrow."[2]

The American public's love for Reagan was strong

INAUGURATION TRADITIONS

The chilly weather on January 21, 1985, forced Reagan to break tradition in several ways. Most previous presidential inaugurations had been held outdoors at the East Portico of the US Capitol. Reagan's was moved indoors. Additionally, almost every president paraded from the Capitol to the White House following the ceremony. Due to extreme cold, the inauguration planners decided to skip the parade. Reagan also helped to change an inaugural tradition with his first inauguration. For the first time, the ceremony was held at the West Front of the Capitol rather than the East Portico. Since that time, each subsequent presidential inauguration has been held at the West Front.

In his second inaugural address, Reagan emphasized the values he carried with him through his political career.

and steady. At the beginning of Reagan's first term, many Americans believed he was a good leader even if they did not agree with all his policies. Admiration for Reagan spanned across generations and political parties. Supporters appreciated his pledge to protect personal freedoms. This dedication to the protection of liberty came at an opportune time. The United States was in the midst of a Cold War with the Soviet Union, a war of ideas rather than outright combat. The Soviet Union's Communist ideology ran counter to Reagan's ideas about individual freedom. Reagan and many other Americans were wary of communism's spread across the globe.

The glamour of inaugural balls would soon give way to
the difficult tasks Reagan faced in his second term.

Reagan promised to put an end to this spread by strengthening the US military. He also promised to uphold what he considered traditional American values. Reagan believed in maintaining an image of a rugged, untamed United States, the United States of the cowboys, where the majesty of rolling hills and open skies still reigned. By making reference to these ideas, Reagan was able to connect with Americans who held the same views.

Ultimately, Reagan would find success in his second term by keeping some of the promises in his inauguration speech while abandoning others. Many observers believe the military buildup he undertook helped to speed the collapse of the Soviet Union, yet Reagan's missile defense system became mired in technical and political issues. While many aspects of the economy improved, the country's poor were sometimes hit hard by Reagan's budget cuts. And a scandal known as the Iran-Contra Affair tarnished the reputation of many within his administration. Through all of these ups and downs, Reagan would maintain his optimism and his steadfast belief, dating back to his youth, that the United States was the greatest nation in the world.

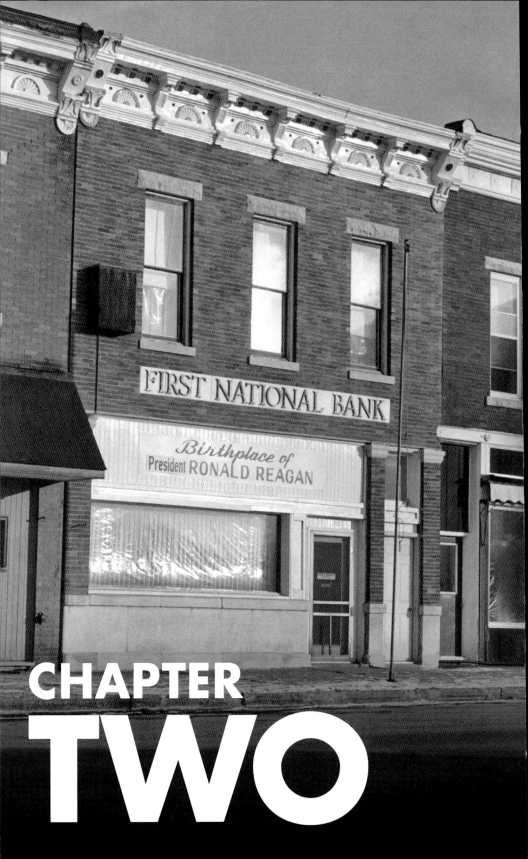

FIRST NATIONAL BANK

Birthplace of
President RONALD REAGAN

CHAPTER
TWO

THE BIRTH OF A PRESIDENT

R onald Reagan was born in Nelle and Jack Reagan's home in Tampico, Illinois, on February 6, 1911. The family lived in an apartment overlooking Main Street. They had no running water and no indoor toilet. Nelle, Ronald's mother, had a difficult labor. She was giving birth at home and there was no doctor around. A midwife was sent to find a doctor in town. With the doctor's help, Ronald was born at 4:16 a.m. The healthy ten-pound (4.5 kg) baby was the Reagans' second son. Their older son, Neil, had been born in September 1908.

Reagan would later cherish his early childhood. He loved hunting, fishing, and spending time in nature. He spent his days swimming with friends, playing football in his neighborhood park, and reading stories with his mother. Reagan's happy childhood helped establish his

Ronald Reagan was born in an apartment above First National Bank in Tampico, Illinois.

view of an idyllic America that later shaped his career as a politician.

Opposites Attract

Nelle and Jack were very different from one another. Nelle was optimistic and trusting. Jack was moody and cynical. Nelle was a devout Protestant with a cheerful demeanor. Jack, on the other hand, was an Irish-Catholic, a chain-smoker, and a heavy drinker. Yet Jack and Nelle shared a strong belief in religious and racial tolerance. Jack hated racial prejudice and refused to stay in hotels that did not admit people of color. Though Ronald loved going to the movies, Jack refused to let his sons watch the popular film *The Birth of a Nation* because it portrayed the Ku Klux Klan, a racist group, in a positive light.

Jack's weakness for drink threatened the family's stability. He was a helpless binge drinker who sometimes went on drinking sprees for days. The family moved frequently, and Nelle hoped the changes would encourage Jack to stop drinking. But when the family settled down in Dixon, Illinois, in 1920, Jack quickly became known as the town drunk. Nelle viewed her

Ronald, *third from left,* appeared on a Christmas card with
his parents and older brother in 1916 or 1917.

husband's alcoholism as a sickness and asked her sons to
support and love their father regardless of his failings.

People remarked on how distant Ronald sometimes
seemed. Although he was always friendly, he also came
across as emotionally guarded. He and his brother
were both aware of the tension under the surface of
their parents' relationship. Additionally, the fact they
moved frequently meant Ronald had a lack of roots and

stable friendships in childhood. As a child, he was quiet and spent a lot of time alone. Still, in his autobiography, Ronald remembered his time in Dixon fondly: "As I look back on those days in Dixon, I think my life was as sweet and idyllic as it could be."[1]

Dixon

In Dixon, Ronald cultivated a love of community, family, and the outdoors. His family remained there for 17 years. Jack persuaded one of his previous employers to help him establish a shoe store in Dixon. He proposed to slowly pay back his former boss through store commissions. Jack marketed the store on the fact that it had a shoe-fitting X-ray machine. At the time, the hazards of radiation were not well known, and shoe salesmen used X-rays to help fit customers' shoes.

Despite the new technology, the sluggish economy meant the store did not get off to a good start.

In 1923, the Reagans moved to another part of town so Ronald could attend the more prestigious North Dixon High School. The Rock River divided Dixon into northern and southern parts. Downtown Dixon was in the southern area and contained many factories. It was home to most of Dixon's working-class Irish-Catholic families. The northern section was the wealthier part of Dixon, and the people who lived there were primarily Protestant.

Neil continued at South Central High School while Ronald started his first year of high school at North Dixon. He liked attending North Dixon because his crush, Margaret Cleaver, was a student there as well. Margaret was the daughter of the minister of Nelle's church. She was a star student at North Dixon. Students at North Dixon tended to be more straitlaced than their South Central counterparts. While students like Neil went to hang out in smoky pool halls, students from the North relaxed in the ice cream parlor. Because classes at North Dixon were tougher, many students would have the chance to attend college. Most students at South Central were expected to get jobs right after high school.

Ronald flourished in high school. He made new friends and pursued new interests. He won the male lead in a school play called *You and I*. Lucky for him, the female lead was his crush, Margaret. During high school, in 1926, Ronald also got a job as a lifeguard at Lowell Park, a park on the Rock River. He continued working as a lifeguard for the next seven summers.

MARGARET CLEAVER

While courting Margaret, Ronald became very close to her father, Ben Cleaver. Ben was a minister and became Ronald's spiritual leader and mentor. He became like a second father to Ronald. Ben taught Ronald about racial equality and opened his eyes to the nonviolent teachings of Mohandas Gandhi.

However, Ben had raised Margaret in a strict, religious household. Soon she became suspicious of Jack Reagan's drinking. When she questioned Ronald about it he worried his father's drinking would jeopardize his relationship with Margaret. He approached his mother about the issue, vowing he would disown his father if he lost Margaret because of Jack's alcoholism. Nelle advised Ronald to be patient with his father and to have faith.

In the end, Margaret decided not to break off her relationship with Ronald due to his father's drinking. Margaret and Ronald dated in high school and college. In his autobiography, Ronald joked the only reason he went to college was to follow Margaret. At the end of their college careers, Ronald gave Margaret a ring and the couple agreed to become engaged. However, the pair moved to different places when they graduated.

Ronald was excited to appear in *You and I* with Margaret Cleaver. Above, they are seated on the couch together. Below, he is kneeling with flowers while she stands before him.

Thanks to his strong swimming skills and ability to act quickly, Ronald saved 77 people from drowning there. Besides rescuing people, he helped teach children how to swim.

In his junior year, Ronald experienced a growth spurt. He grew into a tall, handsome, and personable young man. In his senior year, Ronald began dating Margaret. By the end of high school, in 1928, he was on top of the world. He was a skilled player on his football team, a talented actor, the boyfriend of his dream girl, and class president. Ronald was the picture of an idealistic American boyhood.

CHAPTER
THREE

EARLY DAYS IN EUREKA

In the summer of 1928, Ronald and Margaret packed their bags and made the two-hour drive from Dixon to Eureka College, where Margaret would be attending school. Eureka College was a picturesque institution of learning, with a friendly small-town feel and a campus lined with elm trees. It had originally been a school where people became ministers, but by the late 1920s, Eureka has transformed into a liberal arts college where students could learn about a variety of subjects. It was also the first school in Illinois to admit men and women on an equal basis. Ronald fell in love with it right away.

However, Ronald had no money to attend college. He looked to others for help. Ronald spoke to the dean of Eureka College and explained his situation. He ended up receiving a scholarship that would cover half his tuition. The dean also helped Reagan secure a job washing dishes to help pay any remaining costs. Though

Ronald continued working as a lifeguard through his college years.

Reagan had to work hard to get by, he remembered being happy as a new college student.

Student Strike at Eureka

However, Eureka College was itself in a poor financial situation. Eureka's president, Bert Wilson, began talking about cutting costs by eliminating classes he thought the school did not need. Many students objected to this because it would mean taking away classes some juniors and seniors needed to finish their majors and graduate. Meetings between the school board and Wilson began without giving a thought to the opinion of students and faculty. Desperate, students and faculty created a counterplan to the one Wilson proposed to the board. The board rejected the plan and approved Wilson's. The students and staff then made an appeal asking Wilson to resign.

Ronald, *top right*, with other members of the Eureka College student senate

This was also refused. On the night the board made the final decision to approve Wilson's budget cuts, students and faculty met at midnight in Eureka's chapel to discuss their next move. The students decided to go on strike. Ronald, deeply moved by the events, made a compelling speech about the grievances of the students.

Eureka students launched their strike after Thanksgiving, though they continued to attend athletic practices, religious services, and study sessions. They held dances every afternoon. As a symbol of togetherness, faculty marked the striking students as present. Defeated, President Wilson resigned.

Being involved in this student strike was a significant moment in Ronald's life. He was touched by the solidarity of the students and faculty. Furthermore, it confirmed his worldview, one he would carry with him into his presidency, that good triumphs over evil.

It was while attending Eureka College that the acting bug really bit young Ronald. In the summer after his freshman year, he attended a production of the play *Journey's End* with Margaret and her family. Ronald was entranced by the play's nostalgic depiction

RONALD'S COLLEGE INTERESTS

Though Ronald adored sports and drama, he did not care much for academics. Many of his peers felt he did not apply himself as much as he could have. One of his professors even complained Ronald never opened his books. Margaret encouraged Ronald to study, convinced if he applied himself he could excel. But, preoccupied with acting and sports, he only strived to maintain a C average.

He also found little success on the football field. Though he loved playing, he was not a natural, much to the disappointment of his coach.

Ronald sat on the bench most of his freshman year. While he resented being unable to play football, he continued participating because of his love of the game. His talent for swimming was a consolation for his struggles in football. He worked hard at swimming, winning five events his freshman year and graduating to varsity the following year. However, he still preferred football and aspired to be a star football player. During football games and practices Reagan often joked around and pretended to be a sports announcer, foreshadowing his future career.

of wartime. He strongly identified with the characters. When he returned to Eureka, Ronald joined the Alpha Epsilon Sigma student dramatic society. He appeared alongside Margaret in the play *Aria de Capo*. *Aria de Capo* was entered into a well-respected competition at Northwestern University, located in the suburbs of Chicago, Illinois. Ronald won an acting award for his performance.

Trouble Back Home

Reagan graduated from Eureka College on June 7, 1932. He continued to work as a lifeguard through the summer, but his family was not immune to the economic difficulties of the time. Fashion Boot Shop, the shoe store Jack Reagan had opened in 1921, had closed in 1929, around the start of the Great Depression. Jack went to work at a chain shoe store 150 miles (241 km) from Dixon, and Nelle went to work as a seamstress. As the Depression worsened, the family moved from a rented home to a two-room apartment. Ever the loyal son, Reagan sent home money whenever he could. A painful moment came on Christmas Eve when Jack received a telegram from the shoe store firing him. But despite their extreme poverty, Reagan still remembered his family being extremely close during these times.

At the end of the summer of 1932, Reagan left his longtime job as a lifeguard. During his time working at the river, Reagan had taught many children how to swim. Two of these children belonged to Kansas City businessman Sid Altschuler. Altschuler took a liking to Reagan and now offered to help him find a job. When Reagan told him he wanted to go into radio broadcasting, Altschuler suggested he go to Chicago and try to get any job in radio he could. Inspired by this advice, Reagan hitchhiked to Chicago and visited radio stations asking for work. Unfortunately, there was none to be found, especially for an inexperienced recent college graduate. Station after station told him there were no openings—even seasoned broadcasters were out of work. However, a secretary advised him he might have better luck in places outside of Chicago that were not as well-known for entertainment. Returning home, Reagan was disappointed, but was soon cheered up by his father's offer to let him use his car to look for work in nearby cities.

Reagan looked for a job in Davenport, Iowa, at the WOC radio station. Peter MacArthur, the station

The massive city of Chicago was very different from the small towns where Reagan grew up.

manager, informed him WOC had just recently filled a position for an announcer. Reagan became angry with himself for not approaching WOC earlier. While walking out of MacArthur's office, he muttered about how he could never become a sports announcer if he could not even get a job at a radio station. MacArthur stopped Reagan in his tracks. He asked Reagan if he could announce a football game and Reagan enthusiastically said he could. By himself in the studio, with MacArthur listening, Reagan improvised an imaginary football game broadcast. Impressed by Reagan's skills, MacArthur gave him the opportunity to broadcast a University of Iowa football game the following Saturday. It was the start of Reagan's entertainment career.

Reagan was soon forced to deal with heartbreak when he separated from Margaret. The pair had dated for seven years, staying together through high school and college. After graduation, Margaret went to teach in a school in Cropsley, Illinois. The couple wrote to each other regularly. Yet by May 1933, it was obvious they were drifting apart. In 1933, Margaret traveled to Europe. The following year she wrote Reagan from France to say she had fallen in love with a man in the US Consular Service. Though Reagan was devastated, he kept in mind his mother's philosophy that everything happens for a reason.

A LOCAL HERO

During his time in Iowa, Reagan was a hero to a particular young woman. In 1933, Melba King, a 22-year-old nursing student, was walking home one night when a man with a gun robbed her. Reagan came to the woman's rescue by scaring off the man. He then walked King home. King and Reagan did not see each other again until 1984, when Iowa Governor Terry Branstad invited King to tell her story of Reagan's bravery at a campaign event.

Not long after receiving the news from Margaret, Reagan was confronted with more bad news. His father had suffered a heart attack, leaving him unable to find work. Reagan began sending money home to support his parents while his father was out of work. His love of movies from a young age and his college involvement in drama led Reagan to dream of a career in movies and television. But at the small radio station in Iowa, the chances of these dreams coming true still felt slim.

CHAPTER
FOUR

REAGAN ON THE RADIO

For his first broadcast, Reagan partnered with veteran announcer Gene Loffler to cover a University of Iowa football game. Loffler was a perfect match for Reagan. He was a seasoned broadcaster with limited knowledge of football, while Reagan was an experienced football player with little knowledge of broadcasting. Reagan announced the game enthusiastically and confidently. MacArthur was so impressed by Reagan's performance he invited him to broadcast the remaining three University of Iowa home games and doubled his pay. Early in 1933, MacArthur offered Reagan a job as a staff announcer.

In May 1933, WOC combined with its sister station WHO in Des Moines. Both Peter McArthur and Reagan moved to WHO, and again Reagan's salary doubled. Reagan enjoyed the move because Des Moines was a busier city. At about same time, good news came

Reagan got his first job in the entertainment industry at radio station WOC.

from his parents. Jack had a new job with the Federal Emergency Relief Administration distributing food to the jobless.

From WHO to Hollywood

In 1935, Reagan struck a deal with WHO. He would give up his vacation time if WHO paid for his ticket to travel to Southern California with the Chicago Cubs baseball team for their summer training. He reasoned his broadcasting skills would improve by knowing more about the team. The plan had the added advantage of giving him a lovely summer in sunny California.

A RISING STAR AT WHO

While a broadcaster at WHO, Reagan soon won the hearts of Iowa listeners with his pleasant manner and comforting voice. He developed a style of reading that sounded more like conversation, which made listeners feel like they were listening to a friend. He used this technique later in his life in his presidential speeches.

Ronald soon became a local celebrity and was asked to speak in front of civic and youth groups. This was more good practice for his future in public speaking. He greatly enjoyed the opportunity to personally engage with a large group of people. Reagan went on to become an announcer for a news program featuring Harold Royce Gross, who later became a Republican member of the House of Representatives. The two became friends and frequently got into friendly arguments about Franklin D. Roosevelt—Reagan loved him and Gross hated him.

This first trip began Reagan's lifelong love affair with California.

While in Los Angeles, Reagan reconnected with a former colleague at WHO, Joy Hodges. She had since moved to Hollywood and become a successful singer. Reagan approached her for advice on how to break into the acting industry. Hodges referred Reagan to her agent, George Ward. Ward instantly liked Reagan for his rugged looks. He knew Jack Warner, head of the Warner Brothers film studio, was looking for an actor who fit his description. Ward called Reagan in for a screen test in order to see how he looked on camera. Reagan memorized the script and gave a perfect screen test. Ward tried to convince Reagan to stay in Los Angeles for a few more days so Jack Warner could view his screen test, but Reagan told Ward he had to return to

FAMILY MATTERS

Throughout the time Reagan worked as a broadcaster for WOC and for WHO, he continued to send money back home. This helped his brother Neil pay for his college education at Eureka. It also helped his parents pay their bills during the Great Depression. After Neil graduated, he came to live with Ronald in Des Moines. Ronald used his connections to find Neil some work. Since Neil expressed an interest in working in radio, Ronald helped him get a job at WOC in Davenport—the station had reopened in 1934. In 1936, Neil became the station's program manager.

Des Moines with the Cubs. On his way back home to Iowa, Reagan kicked himself for blowing his chance of becoming an actor. But a few days later, Reagan received a message from Ward saying Warner Brothers was offering him a seven-year contract, starting in 1937. Reagan gladly accepted.

Arriving in Hollywood

After a tearful good-bye from his friends at WHO, Reagan drove west toward his new Hollywood career. He arrived at the Hollywood Plaza Hotel on May 31, 1937. Reagan brought his parents and brother to California within four months, and his life looked a lot like it did in Illinois. He even stayed in touch with his Des Moines fans by writing about his new career for the *Des Moines Sunday Register*. This newspaper column chronicled Reagan's early days in Hollywood. After he finished his first movie, he wrote, "No matter what anyone says or what the future may bring, now I can always insist that I was once an actor."[1]

Reagan was an ideal employee at Warner Brothers due to his good memory of scripts and his willingness to take instructions. Having these skills was like a golden ticket in the entertainment industry, and Reagan quickly

Reagan's successful screen test launched his acting career.

GETTING HIS NAME BACK

From the time Reagan was a boy, he had often used the nickname Dutch. The name was supposedly given to him as a baby by his father, who said the young boy looked like a "fat little Dutchman."[2] The Warner Brothers Company encouraged him not to use his nickname for his film career, believing he should think of something more elegant. When thinking of a screen name, Reagan offered up his given name, Ronald. The studio thought "Ronald Reagan" sounded good, and so Reagan used his given name as an actor.

became an asset to the studio. He acted in many B movies, films made quickly and at low cost, rather than big-budget productions. In most of his films, Reagan was cast as a wholesome, all-American type.

In 1938, Reagan made a total of nine films. That year ended with the making of *Brother Rat*, which received good reviews. In *Brother Rat*, Reagan played a cadet who courted the daughter of his military school's commandant. The actress who played the commandant's daughter was Jane Wyman, Reagan's future wife.

After successful roles alongside stars such as Bette Davis and Humphrey Bogart, Reagan gained the confidence to pursue a wider variety of roles. He sought the role of George Gipp, a famous football player, in the 1940 film *Knute Rockne, All American*. He was interested in the part not only because of his love of sports, but also because he felt the role would help him escape from

One of Reagan's best-known roles was playing football player George Gipp in *Knute Rockne, All American*.

B movies. Warner Brothers was skeptical of giving him the role, but Reagan showed the studio a picture of himself in his old football uniform at Eureka College to convince them he would fit the part. He then approached Pat O'Brien, who would be starring as Knute Rockne. O'Brien was aware of Reagan's athletic background, and he convinced Warner to hire Reagan to play George Gipp. A famous line from the film, "win just one for the Gipper," was later used to promote Reagan during his presidential campaigns. [3]

After *Knute Rockne,* Reagan went on to act in films such as *Santa Fe Trail* (1940) with Errol Flynn and *The Bad Man* (1941) with Wallace Beery and Lionel Barrymore. Making $1,000 a week—a large sum at the time—Reagan had become a star. He then took on the film *King's Row,* a dark, artistic

THE REAL KNUTE ROCKNE

Knute Rockne, All American is about one of the most famous football coaches in history and one of Reagan's idols. Rockne played for the University of Notre Dame's varsity football team and in 1913 became the captain. Upon graduation, Rockne took an assistant coach position and later became head coach. He was Notre Dame's coach from 1918 to 1930. He was known for coaching one of the most beloved football players of all time, George "Gipper" Gipp, who died from disease at a young age. Historians believe Gipp likely died from strep throat—often fatal in the days before modern medicine.

piece. Critics regarded this role as his best performance. However, the timing of the film cast a dark shadow on his acting career. Between the time of its filming in 1941 and its release in 1942, Japan bombed the American naval base at Pearl Harbor, Hawaii. The United States was at war. Reagan had enlisted in the Army Reserve in 1937, and in April 1942 he was ordered into active duty.

CHAPTER
FIVE

FROM ACTING TO POLITICS

Since he had poor eyesight, Reagan was not eligible to fight on the front lines during World War II (1939–1945). He worked on training films and documentaries for his fellow soldiers instead. Reagan claimed he was one of the first to see the atrocities happening in Nazi Germany because he worked with classified films taken in Europe of subjects such as concentration camps.

While serving in the military, Reagan was disturbed by government waste he witnessed. He claimed many of the people who worked for the US military were doing their jobs poorly, yet no one would fire them. He also claimed the US government wasted space by keeping giant warehouses full of useless and outdated documents. After the end of the war in 1945, Reagan's military service ended and he returned to making films.

Reagan was unable to serve in combat during World War II, but he put his acting talents to work creating films for the army.

Before long, Reagan became restless and frustrated with Hollywood. In 1947, he had his first serious dispute with Warner Brothers over being typecast. Reagan commented to a *Los Angeles Mirror* reporter he wanted to start picking his own roles. This prompted Warner to write an angry letter to Reagan. Eventually, Reagan's agent negotiated with Warner so Reagan only had to make one film per year at half the salary. His agent also negotiated a five-year, five-film deal with Universal Studios. This gave Reagan the opportunity to make a range of films, including comedies such as *Bedtime for Bonzo* (1951) and westerns such as *Cattle Queen of Montana* (1954).

Communism and the Screen Actors Guild

During his time in the movie business, Reagan became involved in the Screen Actors Guild (SAG), a labor union representing entertainers. He became very active in the controversy about communism in the film industry, and he was elected president of the Guild in 1947. Reagan believed Joseph Stalin, the leader of the Soviet Union, was trying to make Hollywood an instrument of Communist propaganda. By 1947, the United States had

Reagan testified before the US Congress about
Communist activities in Hollywood.

become involved in a Cold War with the Soviet Union.
The ideological conflict began after the United States
and the Soviet Union worked together to defeat Nazi
Germany in Word War II. After the war, the United
States and the Soviet Union became the two most
powerful nations in the world. Due to their different
political structures, they became highly suspicious of
each other.

At the time, the Soviet Union occupied several
Eastern European countries, worrying anticommunists
in the United States about the potential further spread

of communism. After the destruction brought about by World War II, the United States put into place the Marshall Plan, an economic offer to help European countries get back on their feet. The Soviet Union did not accept it because it did not want the United States to control its economy. A few years after the war, the United States joined with allied nations in Western Europe to establish the North Atlantic Treaty Organization (NATO). NATO vowed to contain the spread of communism, using military force if necessary. In response, the Soviet Union established the Warsaw Pact, allying itself with several Eastern European countries.

The threat of communism became an increasing concern in the United States. There were rumors Communists from the Soviet Union were trying to take over the American film industry. Reagan was still a Democrat like his parents. But it was at this time his public political views began turning more conservative. He was a strong anticommunist advocate and believed communism was the true enemy of the United States.

The Hollywood Couple

When actress Jane Wyman attended a promotional photo shoot in 1938, she did not know she was about to meet her future husband. Both Reagan and Wyman had arrived early, but the photographer was nowhere to be found. Unlike Wyman, Reagan was not irritated by the wait. Wyman was impressed by Reagan's calmness, and the pair began to chat. The two got along right away.

Jane Wyman and Ronald Reagan were married in Glendale, California, on January 26, 1940. The newlyweds moved into Wyman's Beverly Hills

WYMAN'S EARLY LIFE

Jane Wyman was born Sarah Jane Mayfield on January 5, 1917, in Saint Joseph, Missouri. She grew up in a fragmented household. When Wyman was only four years old, her father died of pneumonia. Her mother later went to work in Cleveland, Ohio. Wyman was left in the custody of Richard and Emma Fulks in Saint Joseph. A born performer, Wyman started singing and dancing at the age of ten. In 1932, she dropped out of high school and moved to Hollywood.

Once in Hollywood, Wyman worked as a waitress in a coffee shop while trying to make it as an actress. She claimed she was three years older than she was to get parts. She began as a chorus girl in films such as *The Kid from Spain* (1932), *Elmer the Great* (1933), and *College Rhythm* (1934). She signed a contract with Warner Brothers in 1936. During her time working for Warner Brothers, she met Ronald Reagan.

apartment. On January 4, 1941, Wyman gave birth to baby girl Maureen Elizabeth.

When Wyman and Reagan married, Hollywood was the show business capital of the world. The leaders of the movie industry were looking for perfect marriages to represent an idealized Hollywood. As a result, they focused on the young Reagan family and promoted the Reagans as the perfect couple. Yet the pair was far from perfect. After Jack Reagan died from a series of heart attacks in May 1941, Ronald began to spend more time with his mother and gave less attention to Wyman. Wyman was becoming increasingly ambitious in her acting career while Reagan was getting involved in politics and anticommunist causes.

Yet, despite their difficulties, the Reagans wanted to expand their family. Because Wyman's previous pregnancy was very difficult and because she did not want to put her acting career on hold by becoming pregnant, they decided to adopt a child. On March 18, 1945, the Reagans adopted Michael Edward shortly after he was born to an unwed mother.

In 1947, Wyman discovered she was pregnant again. That same year, Reagan contracted pneumonia and became seriously ill. Jane gave birth to a premature baby

Reagan, Wyman, and their children lived much of their lives in the public eye.

girl on June 26, 1947, and Christine Reagan died one day later. During Jane's delivery and the child's death, Reagan was still in the hospital for pneumonia and could not console Jane in her grief. Friends of the couple suspected the baby was born prematurely due to Jane's stress over her husband's illness. The fact that Wyman and Reagan could not be together during their child's death was very traumatizing. After recovering from the loss of her child, Jane threw herself back into her work. Though Reagan seemed oblivious to the problems in his marriage, the partnership was falling apart. In 1948, Wyman filed for divorce. She was given custody of Maureen and Michael.

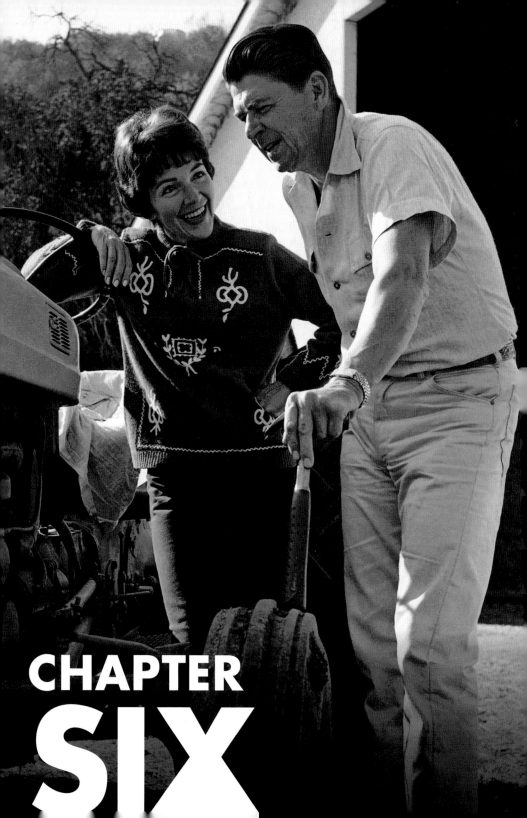

CHAPTER
SIX

BECOMING A GOVERNOR

While president of SAG, Reagan became heavily involved with the issue of communism in Hollywood. He also made it a priority to protect actors who were falsely accused of being Communists. One such actress was Nancy Davis. Davis approached Reagan in 1949 for help disputing an accusation she was a Communist. As it turned out, another actress named Nancy Davis had been accused of Communist leanings. Still, she was very worried the mix-up would tarnish her reputation. To discuss the matter, Reagan and Davis agreed to meet for dinner. Over dinner, both felt a strong connection.

But they did not begin dating right away. Reagan was cautious about falling in love due to the heartbreak of his recent divorce. Yet Davis won Reagan's heart when she became a member of SAG, to which Reagan was very committed. He often spent long nights working at

After marrying Nancy Davis, Reagan began shifting his interests further toward politics.

RONALD AND NANCY'S FIRST DATE

Both Reagan and Nancy were unsure about their relationship on their first date. Both lied and said they could not stay out too late because they had an early film shoot in the morning. However, as the dinner progressed, the pair found themselves captivated in conversation. Reagan liked that Nancy did not just talk about her career, as many other actresses did. She did not simply dream of being a star; she aspired to be a wife and mother and to settle down. Even in her roles as an actress, she was often cast as the responsible young mother. Nancy liked that Reagan talked about his interests. After a long dinner, Reagan invited Nancy out to see a show at Ciro's, a famous nightclub.

SAG headquarters, even poring over paperwork while eating dinner. Davis's involvement in SAG permitted the pair to see each other regularly. During meetings, Davis began to see how Reagan functioned as a leader. Her presence at these meetings marked the beginning of her involvement in Reagan's political life.

The couple began dating in 1950 and had a quiet wedding on March 4, 1952. Seven-and-a-half months later, on October 21, 1952, Nancy gave birth to Patricia Ann Reagan. In honor of his daughter's birth, Reagan planted an olive tree outside of their house.

Throughout their long marriage, the pair had a very strong bond. Over the years, Reagan continuously wrote Nancy love letters. He even claimed he missed her when she left the room. Nancy worked

Reagan on the set of *General Electric Theater* in 1960

hard to help Reagan succeed. He, in turn, adored her and thought she could do no wrong. They were best friends.

General Electric

After their marriage, the couple made significant changes in their lives. Nancy decided to quit her career as an actress to devote herself to life with Reagan. Reagan, disenchanted with Hollywood, decided to turn down movies and work in television instead. In 1954, the General Electric Company asked Reagan to host and occasionally act in a series called *General Electric Theater*. The series presented self-contained stories, often adapted from books or plays. This job would be a personal and professional turning point for Reagan.

General Electric operated many small offices across the country instead of having just one central location. General Electric asked Reagan to travel to these different offices to act as the public face of the company. Soon, Reagan was also being asked to speak at engagements, such as charity events. Instead of telling stories about Hollywood, as was expected, Reagan spoke about his personal beliefs, such as the importance of charitable donations. Reagan later said people he spoke to on these tours believed the government was interfering too much in business. The federal government's overreach became a core belief of Reagan's, and the theme began appearing in his speeches. In the future, it became a major part of his presidential campaign platform. As he would later say as president, he believed "Government's first duty is to protect the people, not run their lives."[1]

Reagan stayed on at *General Electric Theater* for eight years. He looked back fondly on these times as being filled with professional challenges and successes as well as quality time with his family. He and Nancy bought a home overlooking the Pacific Ocean and a ranch in the Santa Monica Mountains. Reagan enjoyed riding his horse and spending time with Nancy and his children. Ronald Prescott, Nancy and Ronald's second and last child, was born on May 20, 1958.

In 1960, after leading SAG in a strike against the Hollywood film studios, Reagan resigned from his post as the group's president. During this time, Reagan furthered his beliefs about government overreach, distrusting the Democratic Party he had once supported. He saw the party as supporting a welfare state rather than personal entrepreneurship. He advocated cutting back on programs such as public education and

NANCY'S EARLY LIFE AND CAREER

Nancy Davis was born in New York City on July 6, 1921. Her parents divorced shortly after her birth. She had been born Anne Frances Robbins, but her name was legally changed when her mother remarried. The family moved to Chicago in 1929. She was very active, playing tennis, swimming, and dancing all through her childhood. She attended Smith College in Massachusetts, where she majored in theatre. Soon after graduation she became a professional actress and moved to New York City.

When Nancy first took the stage, she toured with a road company and then received a role on Broadway in the hit musical *Lute Song*. This led to many other parts, eventually bringing her to Hollywood. Once in California, Nancy made 11 films between 1949 and 1956. Her first role was in *Shadow on the Wall*. Others included *The Next Voice You Hear* and *East Side, West Side*. In 1957, she starred opposite Reagan in *Hellcats of the Navy*.

guaranteed health insurance for the elderly. In 1960, Richard Nixon ran against Democrat John F. Kennedy in the presidential election. Previously, Reagan had voted for Democrats such as Hubert Humphrey and Harry S. Truman. He had also voted against Nixon, a Republican, when Nixon ran for the US Senate in California. But this election was different for Reagan. He began to think the Republican Party was more aligned with his values. After consulting with Ralph Cordiner, the head of General Electric and a Nixon supporter, Reagan decided to give Nixon a chance. He campaigned for Nixon in the 1960 election. Nixon lost, but Reagan increased his visibility on the national political scene. He began sharing his views even more vocally, releasing a spoken-word album in 1961 called *Ronald Reagan Speaks Out Against Socialized Medicine.*

THE REAGAN DEMOCRATS

Reagan had grown up in a family of enthusiastic Democrats. Reagan's parents saw the Democratic Party as the party of the people and as more supportive of the working class than Republicans. Reagan supported Democratic presidential candidate Harry S. Truman in 1948. In 1952 and 1956, he supported Republican candidate Dwight D. Eisenhower for president while remaining a Democrat. In 1960 he again supported a Republican candidate, Richard Nixon, while still a Democrat. Finally, in 1962, Reagan changed his party affiliation to Republican.

The album criticized plans for government health care assistance.

Because of Reagan's increasingly outspoken political views, General Electric fired him in 1962 and canceled *General Electric Theater*. Reagan devoted himself to writing and acted only occasionally. With his new free time, he focused on political activities. In 1964, Reagan was asked to act as cochairman of Republican candidate Barry Goldwater's presidential campaign in California. As cochairman, Reagan traveled around the country making speeches on Goldwater's behalf. His fund-raising campaign was so successful Republican contributors asked him to give a televised speech in favor of Goldwater. The speech would be seen across the country, giving Reagan a chance to launch himself into the national spotlight. This was a big step for both Reagan and Goldwater, and both were nervous about the results of the speech. The speech was titled "A Time for Choosing."

"A Time for Choosing"

In the beginning of his speech, Reagan stated the speech's topic would be controversial. He went on to say he would not apologize for this fact. In the speech,

Reagan hosted events and gave speeches promoting
Barry Goldwater's 1964 presidential campaign.

Reagan advocated for self-governance and described
government as a small group of people who ruled the
destiny of a large group of people. Again emphasizing his
disgust with welfare, Reagan claimed the government
could not control the economy without controlling
people. However, he made clear his belief that all
American citizens had a responsibility to take care of the
less fortunate.

Reagan's main platforms in this speech were tax reform, spending cuts on social welfare programs, and the restoration of the American Dream—which in Reagan's eyes was the opportunity for any individual to succeed. He ended by stating his plans were the answer to the country's problems, even if the answers were simple: "They say we offer simple answers to complex problems. Well, perhaps there is a simple answer — not an easy answer—but simple."[2]

Like Nixon, Goldwater eventually lost his race. But the speech catapulted Reagan into political fame. Many people raved about his persuasive abilities. Though Reagan was himself pleased with the speech, he could not have possibly imagined its influence on his life over the next few decades. Less than 20 years later, he would be taking the oath of office to become the president of the United States.

Republican contributors were incredibly impressed with the speech. To them, Reagan seemed like just the right person to lead the state of California. Shortly after the speech, several Republican officials visited Reagan at his home. They asked him to run for governor of California. At first, Reagan thought this idea was absurd. Why would he make such a radical change in his life?

Reagan's views and proposals made him
popular with many California voters.

He had a stable family and a happy home life, and he felt that was all he needed. But the Republican contributors persisted, saying he was the only person who could put the Republican Party back together again after their election defeats.

Reagan was not convinced. But he made a compromise, agreeing to take a six-month speaking tour of California. As he got out on the road, Reagan held a series of question-and-answer engagements. Reagan started hearing similar grievances to those he had heard when touring for General Electric. People complained about high taxes, high crime rates, air and water pollution, and overregulation of businesses by the government. Many asked him to run for governor. When he came back to California he decided he would make his formal entry into politics.

While running for governor, Reagan maintained that California represented opportunity but had not been living up to its true potential. He ran on an easy-to-understand platform, suggesting if he were to become governor, he would reduce the size of government and cut taxes. Reagan also pledged to quiet the student activists at the University of California's Berkeley campus, forcefully if necessary. The students were protesting against the Vietnam War (1955–1975) and in favor of free speech. Reagan promised to restore traditional values to California. He presented his plan for California as an example the entire nation could follow.

This image instilled hope in many Californians. They were also charmed by the polished appearance Reagan had perfected as an actor. Quick with a joke and able to easily brush off attacks on his inexperience, Reagan presented himself to voters as a regular American. By November 1966, Reagan had won the hearts of Californians and was voted governor of California. He defeated the sitting governor, Pat Brown, by a margin of 1 million votes out of approximately 6 million cast.[3] He was sworn into office on January 2, 1967.

Governor Reagan

However, once he became governor, Reagan seemed to have difficulty adjusting to the position. When asked directly about his policies, Reagan appeared tongue-tied at times. He often avoided questions or turned to an aide for assistance.

Upon entering office, Reagan simultaneously ordered large budget cuts, froze hiring for state agencies, and asked state employees to work without pay on holidays. During Reagan's time as governor he made some seemingly contradictory political moves. He had previously criticized Pat Brown for supporting high taxes, but he doubled state spending in his first term. Also, though he would later take a strong antiabortion stance, Reagan signed a bill lifting many restrictions on abortion in California. When the number of abortions rose, he defended himself to antiabortion voters by claiming his intent was to allow only abortions in rare cases. He claimed women and doctors took advantage of loopholes in the law to perform too many abortions. Reagan spoke firmly against his political opponents, yet negotiated and compromised with them.

It was during his time as governor that Reagan began professional relationships with the political advisers he would work with for the rest of his career. Michael Deaver and Edwin Meese, two members of Reagan's

PAT BROWN

Governor Pat Brown had held office for eight years when Reagan opposed him. During Brown's time in office, he responded to the need for public services by pouring more money into higher education and constructing freeways. Although these measures boosted California's economy and made it more appealing to outsiders, it also resulted in higher taxes. Many Californians were unhappy with the increased tax burden.

Reagan continued campaigning for fellow Republican candidates while governor of California.

California administration, would later become two of his top advisers as president. Deaver would also become a close friend of the Reagans.

By the time his first term was up, Reagan had overcome his early difficulties in the governorship. He was elected for a second term in 1970. This time, his focus was to decrease what he considered to be unnecessary spending on social welfare programs. He tightened restrictions on welfare eligibility. Reagan also emphasized the importance of international relations and encouraged increased imports and exports. However, many economists maintain this plan negatively impacted the state's ability to keep jobs in California rather than sending them overseas. At the end of his second term, Reagan was satisfied with his time as governor. He did not run for a third term in 1974. Instead, he geared up for a presidential run in the upcoming 1976 election.

CHAPTER
SEVEN

PRESIDENT REAGAN

Reagan left his position as governor of California convinced the United States needed a leader to take it in a different direction. Initially, he had planned to run following the end of Nixon's second term as president in 1976. Nixon had won both the 1968 election and reelection in 1972. But the devastating political scandal known as Watergate, in which Nixon's administration was found to have covered up a break-in at a Democratic Party office, resulted in Nixon's resignation in 1974. Vice President Gerald Ford became president when Nixon resigned, leaving Reagan to run against him in 1976. Reagan harshly criticized Ford's policies, as well as the political officials he appointed. But he lost the nomination to become the Republican candidate for president. Ford later lost the election to Democratic candidate Jimmy Carter. Reagan would have to wait four more years, until 1980, for his chance at the office.

Reagan spent the late 1970s preparing for his run for president.

President Jimmy Carter was criticized for his
handling of the Iran hostage crisis.

When 1980 came around, Reagan easily secured
his party's nomination for president. His running mate
was future president George H. W. Bush, who had
been one of Reagan's competitors for the nomination.
Conditions were ripe for Reagan to win the presidency.
The economy was performing poorly. Unemployment
and inflation, key measures of the economy's health,
had risen in the late 1970s. Many blamed Carter.
Additionally, the ongoing Iran hostage crisis hurt
Carter's chances of reelection. Following a revolution
against the US-backed Iranian leader, militants stormed

the US embassy in the Iranian capital of Tehran in November 1979. More than 60 Americans inside the compound were held hostage.[1] The US government was unable to negotiate for their release, and by the time of the 1980 election most were still being held in Iran. Again, popular opinion blamed Carter for his inability to resolve the crisis. A failed rescue attempt by the US Army's elite Delta Force further humiliated the administration and the United States.

In the presidential campaign, Reagan promised to strengthen the country's national defense while at the same time shrinking the role of government. He vowed to bring the United States back into a golden age. To many Americans, Reagan represented an idyllic America that was powerful and

REAGANOMICS

A contributor to the financial magazine *Forbes* has called supply-side economics a "cornerstone of the Reagan Revolution of the 1980s."[2] But Reagan's brand of economic policy—nicknamed Reaganomics—added one important aspect to supply-side economics. In the view of supply-side's inventors, the economy-boosting effects of tax cuts would counteract the deficit created by the government taking in less money. Spending cuts, they believed, would not be necessary. However, Reagan added major spending reductions to the equation, cutting funding for Social Security, food stamps, and health programs for the poor. Despite the reductions, the United States still experienced major budget deficits throughout Reagan's presidency.

confident. For his skill at giving speeches and winning the public's approval, he was nicknamed the "Great Communicator."[3] A famous line from Reagan's closing statement in one of the last presidential debates is still quoted frequently today: "Next Tuesday all of you will go to the polls, will stand there in the polling place and make a decision. I think when you make that decision, it might be well if you would ask yourself, are you better off than you were four years ago?"[4]

On November 4, 1980, most American voters decided they were not better off than they were four years ago, electing Reagan the next president of the United States by a wide margin. Reagan won more than 50 percent of the vote to Carter's 41, with most of the remainder going to third-party candidate John B. Anderson.[5] The period known as the Reagan Revolution had begun.

The First Term

Reagan's presidency began with an early triumph. At a lunch after his inauguration ceremony, he announced the American hostages in Iran had been freed. They had been held for 444 days. With this success, Reagan began implementing the plans he had laid out during his campaign. His wife also took up her own causes.

But a few months later, Reagan's early presidency took a shocking turn. On March 30, 1981, just a few months after Reagan was sworn into office, John Hinckley Jr. attempted to assassinate him. Reagan was leaving a Washington, DC, hotel after giving a speech to union representatives. The hotel had been considered secure, but there was a short distance between the door and Reagan's limousine where he would be exposed to the public at close distance.

Hinckley was obsessed with actress Jodie Foster and believed he could impress her by assassinating the president. As Reagan walked from the hotel to his waiting limousine, Hinckley pulled out a revolver and fired six shots in less than two seconds. A Secret Service agent reacted quickly and pushed Reagan into the car as others attempted to shield the president with their

THE FIRST LADY

Like many recent first ladies, Nancy Reagan championed her own set of causes once she moved to the White House. One of her most significant causes was the "Just Say No" program. The campaign encouraged children to reject drug use, teaching them several ways to "say no" and remove themselves from situations in which they were pressured to use drugs. Nancy Reagan toured the country to spread her message, increasing awareness about the problem of drug use in the United States.

Secret Service agents react to the shooting just after Reagan is shoved into his limousine.

bodies. None of the bullets hit Reagan directly, but the final shot ricocheted off the side of the limousine and struck him on his left side, hitting a rib and stopping near his heart.

Reagan nearly bled to death. However, his good humor in the face of such a serious event endeared him even more to many Americans. He even bantered with the doctors at the hospital, asking them to assure him they were Republicans. One doctor responded, "Today we're all Republicans, Mr. President."[6] Reagan recovered rapidly from the injury, and his humorous reactions to the horrific events made him popular with the public.

Even as he recovered from his injuries, Reagan continued to promote his political positions, including those dealing with the economy. During Reagan's campaign for president, he had advocated for a supply-side economic policy, and the US Congress passed the changes as part of his budget plan in 1981. Under this type of policy, taxes are lowered and economic regulations are removed. The theory is that when people can spend and invest more money, the economy will do better. Reagan's economic policies also included an antiunion stance, which he demonstrated during the air traffic controller strike of August 1981.

AIR TRAFFIC CONTROLLER STRIKE

In August 1981, more than 12,000 air traffic controllers—the airport workers who help guide airplanes through crowded airspace—walked off the job all across the United States.[7] They were striking for better working conditions and increased pay. Since the controllers were federal employees, it was technically illegal for them to go on strike, though other government employees had previously gone on strike without consequences. Reagan ordered the controllers back to work within 48 hours, saying he would fire them if they failed to return to their jobs. Most did not, and Reagan carried through on his threat.

With a lack of air traffic controllers, thousands of flights were canceled. Other air traffic employees and even members of the US military replaced the strikers until new ones could be hired and trained. The events had a lasting impact on unions in the United States. Before 1981, an average of 300 strikes were held per year. Now, the average is less than 30.[8]

The next year the nation slid into a recession, with high unemployment and the largest budget deficits in the nation's history. Reagan supported a tax increase in 1982, and the economy began to recover. Unemployment and inflation dropped, and the economy continued to improve throughout the rest of his presidency.

Reagan believed the United States had grown weak in the 1970s, and he called for large increases in the military budget to fortify the nation's strength. It was the biggest peacetime military buildup in US history. Reagan's goal was to be more aggressive in fighting communism around the world. He took a harsh stance against the Soviet Union, referring to it in a speech as "an evil empire."[9] Some historians have suggested by forcing the Soviet Union to match rapid US increases in defense spending, Reagan helped accelerate the eventual collapse of the Soviet Union.

One of the most significant parts of Reagan's defense planning was the Strategic Defense Initiative, or SDI. The program, introduced in 1983, was a missile defense system. Its goal was to be able to shoot down nuclear missiles in mid-flight. The SDI was criticized both by the Soviet Union, which believed it would destabilize

Reagan addresses the nation about the necessity of the Strategic Defense Initiative.

relations between the two nations, and by scientists, who called it technologically impossible. Because the SDI called for the use of lasers, critics referred to the program as "Star Wars."[10] Nevertheless, Reagan pushed the program forward.

In 1984, Reagan was easily nominated by the Republican Party to serve as its candidate for president again that year. Likewise, George H. W. Bush was selected as the vice presidential candidate. The pair ran against Walter Mondale, who had served as vice president under Carter. Mondale's running mate was Geraldine Ferraro, a US representative from New York

THE REAL "STAR WARS"

The Strategic Defense Initiative program was announced to the nation on March 23, 1983. Under the plan, space-based lasers and other weapons would shoot down enemy missiles before they could hit their targets. Critics charged that the extremely expensive system could easily be defeated. If the enemy sent thousands of decoy bombs along with their real missiles, it could be impossible for the SDI to shoot down the real ones. Many scientists believed the solution to the problem of nuclear war was diplomatic rather than technological. Though Reagan never gave up his support for the SDI, his successor, George H. W. Bush, refocused the program with more limited goals. Rather than attempting to defeat a large-scale attack, it would merely try to shoot down a few missiles sent by terrorists or rogue nations.

and the first woman nominated as a vice presidential candidate by a major party.

The Reagan campaign's message was one of optimism. A famous television advertisement proclaimed "It's morning again in America," suggesting Reagan had helped the nation out of the difficult times it faced during Carter's presidency.[11] The catchphrase also predicted even brighter times were ahead for the United States.

Reagan's quips continued to make him popular with voters. When asked at a debate against Mondale whether his age, 73, would make the duties of the presidency difficult for him, Reagan responded, "I will not make age an issue of this campaign. I am not going to exploit, for political purposes,

Reagan's strong performances in the presidential debates helped carry him to a second term.

my opponent's youth and inexperience."[12] Even Mondale laughed at the joke.

On November 6, 1984, Americans voted overwhelmingly for Reagan and Bush. The incumbents were victorious by more than 18 percentage points in the popular vote, winning every state except Minnesota, Mondale's home state.[13] Reagan's second term began on a high. It would end up filled with both controversy and progress.

CHAPTER
EIGHT

AT A CROSSROADS

Reagan's second term provided him with a chance to extend his existing policies and present new ones. In his first term, Reagan had started an economic policy emphasizing tax cuts, reductions in domestic spending, and a balanced budget. But he received criticism for his domestic spending cuts because they mostly affected poor Americans.

At the same time, the media published photographs of lavish parties the Reagans threw even as the nation went through recession. Reporters snapped photographs of fashionable men and women darting in and out of the White House in diamond-studded dresses and expensive suits. The media portrayed Reagan and Nancy as callous and insensitive in the face of poorer Americans' struggles.

A Position of Strength

Although Reagan continued a military buildup, his second term saw a thawing of the relations between the

Reagan writes his second inaugural address in his study.

Reagan's 1985 meeting with Gorbachev signaled improving relations between the United States and the Soviet Union.

United States and the Soviet Union. His anticommunist speeches became less harsh, and he encouraged the reforms beginning to take hold in the Soviet Union. The improvement in relations led to a major summit with Mikhail Gorbachev, the leader of the Soviet Union. The pair first met in Geneva, Switzerland, in November 1985 to discuss possible reductions in each side's arsenal of nuclear weapons.

The two men strolled around the grounds of the French consulate in Geneva and discussed the state of the world. They decided both would make a serious effort to halt the continued expansion of nuclear weapons. The men knew it was a major problem with no easy answers, but both Gorbachev and Reagan had clear reasons for pursuing a solution. Reagan wanted to put an end to the threat of communism, while Gorbachev wanted to be on good terms with the United States so he could focus on issues within the Soviet Union instead. After their meeting, each commented on the other's warmth of character. A subsequent summit in Iceland in 1986 was stalled by disagreements over the SDI, but

A NEW KIND OF LEADER

Mikhail Gorbachev is best known for his innovative foreign initiatives. He earned a law degree from Moscow University, where he joined the Communist Party. During this time, he also became secretary of the law department's Young Communist League. He then went on to study agriculture and economics.

When Gorbachev became general secretary of the Soviet Union he began to make reforms to the Soviet system. He permitted freedom of expression that had not been present for many years in the Soviet Union. Furthermore, he stopped intervening in Communist conflicts around the world. Without the support of the Soviet Union, many of the Communist countries were unable to expand. Gorbachev also withdrew Soviet forces from Central Europe.

Throughout his career, Gorbachev continued to press for the democratization of the Soviet Union and permitted free elections in Russia. His reforms led to the downfall of the Soviet Union. In 1990, he was awarded the Nobel Peace Prize for his approach to foreign policy.

a December 1987 meeting in Washington, DC, was a success, leading to the removal of some nuclear weapons from Europe. For the first time, a nuclear weapons treaty required an actual reduction in the number of weapons, rather than simply limiting the production of new ones.

Despite his softer approach to the Soviet Union, Reagan continued making efforts to assist anticommunist movements around the world. The morality and lawfulness of these actions was sometimes called into question. In the name of countering communism, Reagan supported a number of dictators in the developing world. These included figures such as Ferdinand Marcos in the Philippines, whose presidency was marked by widespread government corruption, and Jean-Claude Duvalier in Haiti, who authorized the mass killing and torture of Haitians. Reagan backed Iraqi dictator Saddam Hussein, supporting him in his war against Iran despite his use of poison gas against Iranian troops and civilians. After a Soviet invasion of Afghanistan in 1979, Reagan supported anti-Soviet fighters known as the mujahideen. Many of the same fighters later fought the forces of the United States after its own invasion of Afghanistan in 2001.

Reagan met with mujahideen leaders at the Oval Office of the White House.

The Iran-Contra Affair

Reagan supported similar aid in the Central American country of Nicaragua. In 1979, a group known as the Sandinista National Liberation Front took over Nicaragua's government. The new government sided with Cuba and other Communist countries. In the eyes of the Reagan administration, this was a threat to the United States. In 1981, the US government sent $20 million to fund anti-Sandinista guerilla fighters known as "Contras."[1] Though the Contras were not strong enough to completely overthrow the government, they caused severe damage with their repeated attacks.

THE SANDINISTAS AND THE CONTRAS

The Sandinista National Liberation Front was established in 1961. Inspired by the Cuban Revolution, the Sandinistas aimed to rid Nicaragua of military dictatorship. They were dissatisfied with the state of Nicaragua under its leader at the time. They also resented US intervention in Nicaraguan affairs.

The Contras, on the other hand, were a group of right wing paramilitary organizations committed to overthrowing the Sandinista National Liberation Front. Though many of the Contras' member organizations had similar aims, they did not always work together. Two of the main groups were called the Nicaraguan Democratic Force and the United Nicaraguan Opposition.

Reagan had given his public support to the Contras, praising the fighters and their struggle: "They are the moral equal of our Founding Fathers and the brave men and women of the French Resistance. We cannot turn away from them, for the struggle here is not right versus left; it is right versus wrong."[2]

In November 1985, Reagan approved a secret plan to sell weapons and equipment to Iran in exchange for the release of American hostages in Lebanon. Because Iran had been declared a state sponsor of terrorism, the sales went against the administration's own policy. When the news of the sales came out to the public in 1986, Reagan was deeply embarrassed. But the worst of the controversy was yet to come.

Reagan claimed in a 1987 press conference that he never deliberately lied to the public about the Iran-Contra Affair.

Soon after the release of the weapons-for-hostages news, it was revealed some of the money from the sales had gone to purchase equipment for the Contra fighters in Nicaragua. Under a law passed in 1984, the sending of American aid to the Contras was illegal. The incident became known as the Iran-Contra Affair. Reagan fired the officials who had directly participated in the redirection of money and ordered a full investigation. No evidence was found linking Reagan to the incident, but he accepted full responsibility. His public approval ratings fell in the immediate aftermath of the crisis, but they eventually began to slowly recover.

Taking Down the Wall

On June 12, 1987, Reagan addressed the people of West Berlin, Germany, challenging Gorbachev to tear down the wall dividing Communist East Berlin from West Berlin. In a speech before the Brandenburg Gate in Berlin, Reagan proclaimed, "General Secretary Gorbachev, if you seek peace, if you seek prosperity for the Soviet Union and Eastern Europe, if you seek liberalization: Come here to this gate! Mr. Gorbachev, open this gate! Mr. Gorbachev, tear down this wall!"[3]

The Berlin Wall was a strong symbol of the Cold War, reflecting the division between Communist and Democratic

Reagan's speech was held to commemorate the 750th anniversary of the city of Berlin.

countries. However, it was not until November 9, 1989, that Reagan's words were heeded and the Berlin Wall was taken down. At the end of December 1991, Gorbachev dissolved the Soviet Union for good. Though the change occurred years after Reagan left office, many believe Reagan's staunch anticommunist actions and military buildup contributed to the downfall of the Soviet Union. Some also credit Reagan's series of long and personal meetings with Gorbachev.

CHAPTER
NINE

A QUIET RETIREMENT

Upon leaving the White House in January 1989, Ronald Reagan returned to California. He retired to the wealthy Bel Air neighborhood of Los Angeles. He left the nation in the hands of his former vice president, George H. W. Bush. After his presidency, Reagan spent time working on his ranch, playing golf, visiting friends, and making public appearances. He was one of the highest-paid public speakers at the time, receiving millions of dollars just for a few minutes of speaking. Reagan gave a well-received speech at the 1992 Republican National Convention.

Reagan spent time working on a memoir, which he published in 1990, titled *An American Life*. He also oversaw the creation of the Ronald Reagan Presidential Library in Simi Valley, California. For his achievements in office, Reagan was awarded the Presidential Medal of Freedom by his successor, President George H. W.

Reagan and George H. W. Bush remained friends after Reagan left office in 1989.

LIFE AFTER THE PRESIDENCY

Reagan continued to be active during the early part of his retirement. After his presidency he was in high demand as a public speaker and traveled to places from Japan to Poland to England to speak to large groups of people. On June 14, 1989, he was presented with a knighthood by Queen Elizabeth II. On July 21, 1989, Reagan was inducted into the National Cowboy Hall of Fame in Oklahoma City, Oklahoma. He was also awarded a medal by the Japanese government in October 1989.

Bush, on January 13, 1993. His last significant public appearance was at the funeral of former president Richard Nixon in April 1994.

News of Illness

Reagan's peaceful retirement was shattered by a life-changing announcement. On November 5, 1994, Reagan addressed a letter to the American public. It began, "My fellow Americans, I have recently been told that I am one of the millions of Americans who will be afflicted with Alzheimer's disease."[1] In his letter, Reagan described the heavy burden this degenerative brain disease would place upon his wife, Nancy, and wished he could spare her from its pain. He ended the letter stating, "I now begin the journey that will lead me into the sunset of my life. I know that for America there will always be a bright

Reagan's November 22, 1994, visit to his presidential library was his first public appearance since revealing his diagnosis of Alzheimer's disease.

dawn ahead. Thank you, my friends. Sincerely, Ronald Reagan."[2]

After announcing he had Alzheimer's disease, Reagan largely stayed out of public view. As the disease's symptoms grew more pronounced, Nancy Reagan became increasingly protective of her husband and his public image. She did not want the American public to see his vulnerability or his suffering. On October 31, 1995, the couple announced the creation of the Ronald and Nancy Reagan Research Institute, dedicated to the study of Alzheimer's disease.

ALZHEIMER'S DISEASE

Alzheimer's disease is a degenerative brain disease. This means it becomes worse as it continues and always leads to death. It affects people's memory gradually, until eventually they are unable to recall even the most basic details and recognize their closest loved ones.

Though memory loss is the best-known symptom of Alzheimer's disease, it is not the only one. The disease also harms other functions controlled by the brain, including language and motor skills. Muscles shrink from disuse, leaving sufferers unable to get out of bed or feed themselves. The person's mood becomes unstable as the disease progresses to the stage of dementia. Finally, the person stops responding and loses control over bodily functions. Death generally follows soon after.

Although there is no cure for Alzheimer's disease, scientists have developed treatments that can improve and prolong the life of patients who suffer from it. It is also believed a healthy diet and exercise can decrease the risk of developing the disease in the first place.

Nancy Reagan pauses to kiss her husband's casket as it lies in the US Capitol building.

Reagan suffered a fall in January 2001, breaking his hip. The next month, he turned 90 years old, becoming only the third former president to reach that age. Few visitors were allowed to see Reagan in his final few years. After ten years of fighting Alzheimer's disease, Ronald Reagan died on June 5, 2004. He was given a state funeral. International leaders, Republicans, Democrats, and thousands of ordinary American citizens paid their respects to his legacy. He was buried on the grounds of the Ronald Reagan Presidential Library.

Legacy

Reagan's presidency remains highly controversial. He was a hero to some and a villain to others. President George H. W. Bush and his successor, Bill Clinton, both had to deal with the large budget deficit Reagan left behind. Further, some critics felt the idyllic picture of America Reagan presented in his campaigns and speeches was unrealistic and ignored poverty and racism. Other critics believed Reagan knew more about the Iran-Contra Affair than was released to the public.

Still, Reagan left office with an approval rating of more than 60 percent.[3] He cultivated an image of himself as an average American. His self-deprecating humor, his traditional values, and his pride for the United States struck a chord with millions of

Americans. Reagan's way with words was superb, making him one of the best-regarded public speakers in American history. In terms of policy, some believe his actions sped up the downfall of the Soviet Union.

Ronald Reagan is remembered for his devotion to the United States and his commitment to protecting its interests. His unwavering dedication to creating a brighter future for the nation was inspiring to millions. To this day, he remains a symbol of American optimism.

TIMELINE

1911
Ronald Reagan is born in Tampico, Illinois, on February 6.

1928
Reagan graduates from North Dixon High School in Illinois.

1932
Reagan graduates from Eureka College.

1933
Reagan becomes a sports announcer for the radio station WHO in Des Moines, Iowa.

1937
Reagan signs a seven-year contract with Warner Brothers.

1940
Reagan marries actress Jane Wyman on January 26.

1942

In April, Reagan reports to Fort Mason,
California for active duty in the army.

1947

Reagan is elected president of the Screen Actors Guild.

1948

Reagan and Jane Wyman divorce.

1952

Reagan marries Nancy Davis on March 4.

1960

Reagan resigns from the Screen Actors Guild
and becomes more involved in politics.

1964

Reagan's speech in support of Barry Goldwater,
"A Time for Choosing," airs on television.

1967

Reagan is inaugurated as governor of California.

TIMELINE

1976
Reagan runs for president but fails to win the Republication nomination.

1980
Reagan is elected the fortieth president of the United States.

1981
Reagan survives an assassination attempt on March 30.

1983
Reagan announces his proposal for the Strategic Defense Initiative.

1984
In the presidential election, Reagan defeats Walter Mondale in a landslide.

1986
The Iran-Contra Affair is made public.

1987

Reagan gives his famous "tear down this wall" speech in West Berlin.

1989

Reagan leaves the presidency and returns to California.

1992

Reagan gives a well-received speech at the Republican National Convention.

1994

On November 5, Reagan announces in a letter to the American public he has been diagnosed with Alzheimer's disease.

2004

On June 5, Reagan dies at age 93.

ESSENTIAL FACTS

Date of Birth
February 6, 1911

Place of Birth
Tampico, Illinois

Date of Death
June 5, 2004

Parents
Nelle Wilson Reagan and John Edward Reagan

Education
North Dixon High School; Eureka College

Marriage
Jane Wyman (January 26, 1940–1948)
Nancy Davis (March 4, 1952)

Children
With Jane Wyman, daughter Maureen Elizabeth and adopted son Michael Edward. Daughter Christine died after one day. With Nancy Davis, daughter Patricia Ann and son Ronald Prescott.

Career Highlights
After a successful career as an actor in B movies, Reagan is hired to host a television show called *General Electric Theater*.

Reagan later gives a television address supporting Republican presidential candidate Barry Goldwater that launches his political career and leads to his governorship of California. On November 4, 1980, Reagan is elected president of the United States and holds office for two consecutive terms.

Societal Contributions

While serving in the Army Air Forces, Reagan makes more than 400 training films. In a Washington summit, Reagan and Gorbachev sign the first US-Soviet treaty committed to the destruction of nuclear weapons. Many attribute the Soviet Union's collapse to Reagan's military buildup. Following his presidency, he uses his fame to raise awareness about Alzheimer's disease.

Conflicts

After entering office in difficult economic times, the United States under Reagan falls into a severe recession. On November 13, 1986, Reagan admits he sent defensive weapons to Iran. An investigation concludes Reagan's lax style of management enabled his staff to trade arms to Iran in exchange for hostages and to illegally pursue a secret war against the Nicaraguan government.

Quote

"In this blessed land, there is always a better tomorrow."
—*Ronald Reagan*

GLOSSARY

chronicled
Wrote an account of events.

communism
An economic system based on the elimination of private ownership of factories, land, and other means of economic production.

deregulation
The removal of legal restrictions from an industry.

entrepreneurship
The development and management of one's own business.

guerrilla fighter
A small group of fighters who are not part of a regular army and who use unconventional tactics.

idyllic
Happy and peaceful.

inauguration
A ceremony marking the entrance of a president into office.

incumbent
The current officeholder.

inflation
An increase in prices and a decrease in the purchasing value of money.

picturesque
Beautiful.

pneumonia
A disease caused by bacteria or viruses in the lungs.

portico
A roofed, open-air structure attached to a building.

propaganda
Misleading information used to influence public opinion.

solidarity
Support for an idea or cause.

typecast
To cast repeatedly in only one particular kind of acting role.

welfare
Money or goods given by the government with the intention of helping society's poorest people.

ADDITIONAL RESOURCES

Selected Bibliography

Cannon, Lou. *Governor Reagan: His Rise to Power.* New York: Public Affairs, 2003. Print.

Reagan, Ronald. *The Reagan Diaries.* New York: Harper, 2007. Print.

Further Readings

Burgan, Michael. *Ronald Reagan (DK Biography).* New York: DK, 2011. Print.

Milton, Joyce. *Who Was Ronald Reagan?* New York: Grosset & Dunlap, 2005. Print.

Web Sites

To learn more about Ronald Reagan, visit ABDO Publishing Company on the World Wide Web at **www.abdopublishing.com**. Web sites about Ronald Reagan are featured on our Book Links page. These links are routinely monitored and updated to provide the most current information available.

Places to Visit

Rancho del Cielo
217 State Street
Santa Barbara, California 93101
http://www.yaf.org/TheReaganRanch.aspx
Rancho del Cielo, now known as Reagan Ranch, was one
of Reagan's most beloved properties. It is maintained by the
Young America's Foundation.

Ronald Reagan Boyhood Home and Visitors Center
816 South Hennepin Avenue
Dixon, IL 61021
815-288-5176
http://reaganhome.org
The site of Ronald Reagan's boyhood home has been
preserved and is now open to visitors.

Ronald Reagan Presidential Foundation and Library
40 Presidential Drive
Simi Valley, CA 93065
805-522-2977
http://www.reaganfoundation.org
The Ronald Reagan Presidential Foundation and Library
contains galleries and exhibits dedicated to honoring
Reagan's life and work. It also houses Reagan's presidential
records, more than 60 million pages of documents, tens
of thousands of audiotapes, and more than 1 million
photographs.

SOURCE NOTES

Chapter 1. The Second Inaugural

1. "Second Inaugural Address of Ronald Reagan." *The Avalon Project*. Yale Law School, 2008. Web. 12 Mar. 2013.

2. Ibid.

Chapter 2. The Birth of a President

1. Ronald Reagan. *An American Life*. New York: Pocket, 1990. Print. 29.

Chapter 3. Early Days in Eureka

None.

Chapter 4. Reagan on the Radio

1. Ronald Reagan. *An American Life*. New York: Pocket, 1990. Print. 86.

2. "Reagan Quotes." *Ronald Reagan*. Eureka College, 2013. Web. 12 Mar. 2013.

3. "Knute Rockne's 'Win One for the Gipper' Speech." *University of Notre Dame Archives*. University of Notre Dame, n.d. Web. 12 Mar. 2013.

Chapter 5. From Acting to Politics

None.

Chapter 6. Becoming a Governor

1. "Remarks at the National Conference of the Building and Construction Trades Department, AFL-CIO." *University of Texas Archives*. University of Texas, n.d. Web. 12 Mar. 2013.

2. "A Time for Choosing." *PBS*. WGBH Educational Foundation, 2010. Web. 12 Mar. 2013.

3. "CA Governor 1966." *Our Campaigns*. Our Campaigns, n.d. Web. 12 Mar. 2013.

Chapter 7. President Reagan

1. "Iran Hostage Crisis." *Encyclopaedia Britannica*. Encyclopaedia Britannica, 2013. Web. 12 Mar. 2013.

2. Brian Domitrovic. "Ignorance Abounds About Supply-Side Economics." *Forbes*. Forbes, 11 Dec. 2012. Web. 12 Mar. 2013.

3. "Ronald W. Reagan." *Encyclopaedia Britannica*. Encyclopaedia Britannica, 2013. Web. 12 Mar. 2013.

4. Michael De Groote. "Ronald Reagan's 10 Best Quotes." *Deseret News*. Deseret News, 7 Feb. 2011. Web. 12 Mar. 2013.

5. "1980 Presidential General Election Results." *US Election Atlas*. David Leip, 2012. Web. 12 Mar. 2013.

6. Bob Schieffer. "The Reagan Shooting: A Closer Call Than We Knew." *CBS News*. CBS News, 27 Mar. 2011. Web. 12 Mar. 2013.

7. Kathleen Schlach. "1981 Strike Leaves Legacy for American Workers." *NPR News*. NPR, 3 Aug. 2006. Web. 12 Mar. 2013.

8. Ibid.

9. "Ronald W. Reagan." *Encyclopaedia Britannica*. Encyclopaedia Britannica, 2013. Web. 12 Mar. 2013.

10. Ibid.

11. "Top 10 Campaign Ads." *Time*. Time, 2013. Web. 12 Mar. 2013.

SOURCE NOTES CONTINUED

12. M. J. Stephey. "Top 10 Memorable Debate Moments." *Time*. Time, 2013. Web. 12 Mar. 2013.

13. "1984 Presidential General Election Results." *US Election Atlas*. David Leip, 2012. Web. 12 Mar. 2013.

Chapter 8. At a Crossroads

1. "Ronald W. Reagan." *Encyclopaedia Britannica*. Encyclopaedia Britannica, 2013. Web. 12 Mar. 2013.

2. Gerald M. Boyd. "Reagan Terms Nicaraguan Rebels 'Moral Equal of Founding Fathers.'" *New York Times*. New York Times, 2 Mar. 1985. Web. 12 Mar. 2013.

3. "Ronald Reagan Remarks at the Brandenburg Gate." *American Rhetoric*. American Rhetoric, 2013. Web. 12 Mar. 2013.

Chapter 9. A Quiet Retirement

1. "Primary Resources: Alzheimer's Letter." *PBS*. WGBH Educational Foundation, 2010. Web. 12 Mar. 2013.

2. Ibid.

3. "Presidential Approval Ratings—Gallup Historical Statistics and Trends." *Gallup*. Gallup, 2013. Web. 12 Mar. 2013.

INDEX

INDEX CONTINUED

ABOUT THE AUTHOR

Rosa Boshier is a writer, artist, and educator residing in San Francisco, California. She works in the nonprofit sector as a grant writer and a development consultant. She has been a contributing writer to several arts and culture blogs throughout California in the past seven years.